Winning Ways
Inspiration for Uncommon Living

Tom Goodman

FOR MOM

Unless otherwise noted, Scripture quotations are from the Holy Bible, New International Version, copyright © 1973, 1978, 1984 by International Bible Society. Scriptures marked (NLT) are from the Holy Bible. New Living Translation, copyright © 1996 by Tyndale Charitable Trust. Scriptures marked (GNT) are from the Good News Translation), copyright © 1992 from the American Bible Society. Scriptures marked (NKJV) are from the Holy Bible, New King James Version, copyright © 1982 by Thomas Nelson, Inc.

Copyright © 2018 Tom Goodman
All rights reserved.
ISBN-10: 1984057170
ISBN-13: 978-1984057174

40 DAYS

According to the Bible, a lot can take place in forty days. Noah's entire world was changed by forty days of rain. Moses spent forty days on Mount Sinai and came back with the Ten Commandments. Israel's spies spent forty days in the Promised Land. A shepherd boy named David had enough after forty days of Goliath's taunts. God sustained his prophet Elijah for forty days on a single meal. The pagan city of Nineveh repented when given forty days to do so. Jesus himself was prepared for his life's work after forty days in the wilderness. And the disciples were prepared for their life's work after spending forty days with Jesus after his resurrection.

What could happen to your life in just forty days?

Let's find out! In these pages you'll find inspiration for uncommon living. Pick a day to start, and let this book guide you into deeper fellowship with God.

TABLE OF CONTENTS

DAY 1 SHOCKING REVELATION!.. 1
DAY 2 GOD'S POWER FOR YOUR LIFE 3
DAY 3 CLEANLINESS REALLY IS NEXT TO GODLINESS... 5
DAY 4 THE NÛN AND THE NONES 7
DAY 5 THE POWER OF YOUR EXPECTATIONS 9
DAY 6 NO MORE HERMIT HOLES 11
DAY 7 AGENTS FOR PEACE IN A DIVERSE WORLD 13
DAY 8 A HEARTLESS CRIME 15
DAY 9 DISCOVER HOPE... 17
DAY 10 MEET EL ROI 19
DAY 11 GOD'S FORWARD OBSERVERS 21
DAY 12 FOUNDATIONS... 23
DAY 13 SWEET TEA FOR THE SOUL... 25
DAY 14 "WE MUST HAVE THEE, O JESUS OF THE SCARS" 27
DAY 15 WHO GOD SAYS YOU ARE.. 29
DAY 16 WHO'S ON YOUR FRIDGE?.. 31
DAY 17 BENCHMARKS OF SPIRITUAL GROWTH................ 33
DAY 18 OBJECTS IN MIRROR ARE CLOSER THAN THEY APPEAR... 35
DAY 19 THE MOST IMPORTANT WORD YOU'LL LEARN THIS WEEK 37
DAY 20 TO FORBEAR IS DIVINE 39
DAY 21 DON'T LOOK BACK 41
DAY 22 FIT YOUR STORY INTO GOD'S BIGGER STORY ... 43
DAY 23 GOOD RIDDANCE DAY 45
DAY 24 YOUR WORK MATTERS TO GOD................................ 47

DAY 25 TEACH US TO NUMBER OUR DAYS	49
DAY 26 LONGING FOR LIGHT	51
DAY 27 A BROKEN WORLD AND A GOOD GOD	53
DAY 28 ARE YOU AFRAID TO WIN?	55
DAY 29 WHY YOU EXIST	57
DAY 30 PROOF OF LIFE	59
DAY 31 SAINTS ALIVE!	61
DAY 32 A CRIPPLE AT THE KING'S TABLE	63
DAY 33 EDGING GOD OUT	65
DAY 34 HERE I AM	67
DAY 35 LOL WITH GOD	69
DAY 36 SOLVING A "CRITICAL" PROBLEM	71
DAY 37 ANGER MANAGEMENT"	73
DAY 38 PASSION AGAIN	75
DAY 39 WHAT IMPRESSION ARE YOU MAKING?	77
DAY 40 TRUSTING GOD'S ABUNDANCE	79
ABOUT THE AUTHOR	81

DAY 1
SHOCKING REVELATION!

A routine of daily prayer and meditation is tough to develop. In fact, we'd rather apply electric shocks to ourselves than sit alone and think.

That's the finding of a widely reported study published in *Science* magazine. When psychologists asked people to sit alone with their thoughts and report on the experience, few liked it. But would people so dislike sitting inactive that they'd rather engage in a mildly unpleasant activity? To find out, researchers left people alone in a room with nothing but an electrical shock device. Two-thirds of men and a quarter of women preferred to administer tiny jolts to themselves rather than do nothing. The average was about 7 times in 15 minutes, though one man managed 190 zaps in that time frame.

Blaise Pascal would not have been surprised. He was a famous 17th century mathematician and philosopher—and a passionate Christian. He wrote, "If our condition were truly happy we should feel no need to divert ourselves from thinking about it." Without distractions, we're forced to examine the worth of our assumptions and behaviors and priorities. Maybe that's why even those of us who are Christians prefer to start our day with our mobile devices instead of our Bibles.

But Jesus often withdrew from the crowd for private prayer (Matthew 26:36, Luke 9:18). If he found benefit from it, surely those who follow him will. This 40-day trip you've begun toward uncommon living will require you to spend a little time alone with your thoughts each day. It's not as easy as it seems. "Silence is for bumping into yourself," a monk tells George Prochnik, the author of *In Pursuit of Silence: Listening for Meaning in a World of Noise*. We don't always find ourselves good company.

Here's how I do it. I try to begin my day with a reading from Scripture. I reflect on the text until I can answer three questions:

What do I need to praise God for?
What do I need to confess?
What do I need to ask God for?

It's a simple routine to practice, but over time the results can be profound. Through this practice across the years I've uncovered assumptions I needed to change, or rebellions I needed to surrender, or new roads I needed to take.

Spend some time alone with God today. You may be—um—shocked at what you discover!

Read: Psalm 119:9-16.
Think: How does hiding God's word in our heart help us deal with sin?
Pray: "What do I need to praise God for? What do I need to confess? What do I need to ask God for?" Turn these three questions into prayer requests.

DAY 2
GOD'S POWER FOR YOUR LIFE

"Is God there?" a child's voice asked. "I want to talk to God."

People began leaving requests to talk to God on the answering machine at Radio Colorado Network after the release of the film *Bruce Almighty*. In the film, God repeatedly leaves his phone number on the lead character's pager. It turns out that the Network shared the same number.

Some messages were funny, like the caller who recorded, "I know this isn't the number for God. But I'm calling to see if you have the other number."

Some messages were touching, like the woman who left the message: "I'm in jail right now. Like I said to you last night, 'I love you,'" she confided to God, after promising to go straight and praying to return to her husband and children.

The Radio Colorado Network wasn't the only recipient of requests to talk to God. The phone number is assigned to phone customers in more than 30 area codes, many of whom received calls to God in the weeks after the film's release. One was a church in Sanford, North Carolina. Callers got to talk to a pastor.

Named Bruce.

Thankfully, it doesn't take a phone number to talk to God. In Psalm 34:18, King David promised, "The Lord is close to the brokenhearted and saves those who are crushed in spirit."

I was taught an outline for prayer using the acrostic "P-R-A-Y."

Praise: Take a moment at the start of prayer to recall God's character and promises, and thank him for his activity in your life.

Repent: Confess to God the attitudes and behavior that you know have grieved him. Trust that "he is faithful and just and will forgive us our sins and purify us from all unrighteousness" when we repent (1 John 1:9).

Ask: Bring your needs to God. Don't decide ahead of time what you feel he's capable of granting or what he might regard as "worthy" for a prayer request. Just talk to him.

Yield: We should accept God's will for our lives, trusting that whatever he does with our prayer requests is part of his perfect will for us.

So, p-r-a-y. Talk to him about what your burdens and trust that he is at your side. No phone number required!

Read: Psalm 34:17-18
Think: We may be faithful at lifting up our requests to God. But when was the last time you asked others to pray for you?
Pray: Ask a bold request of God today. Don't calculate ahead of time if it's a reasonable request to ask. Just lift it to God.

DAY 3
CLEANLINESS REALLY IS NEXT TO GODLINESS

It's interesting how we humans make a fundamental link between guilt and washing. Psychological studies bear this out.

"Showering –a simple everyday activity – is linked to morality in a way we never knew," said Katie Liljenquist of Northwestern University.

Liljenquist and her colleagues asked a group of 60 college students to concentrate on either something ethical or unethical that they had done in the past. The researchers discovered that students who remembered their own unethical behavior were more likely to act as if they felt unclean.

For example, the students were given the word "W_ S H" and asked to complete the letters. Students who reflected on an unethical memory were more likely to say that the unfinished word was "WASH" instead of "WISH."

Again, when given the word "S O _ P" they completed the letters as "SOAP" instead of "SOUP."

In another similar experiment, after students were asked to remember some ethical or unethical action from their past, each student was given a choice of two free gifts: a pencil, or an antiseptic wipe. Sixty-six percent of the students who said they had recalled an unethical memory took the antiseptic wipe. It was as if they wanted to wipe themselves clean of the recollection.

It's a common impulse, universal across the cultures. When King David called out to God in confession of his adultery, he cried, "Wash away all my iniquity and cleanse me from my sin" (Psalm 51:2).

It's good to know God responds to that kind of heart cry. In fact, the Bible often reminds us that the blood of Jesus washes out the shame and stain of our sins. Revelation 7:14, for example, speaks of believers who "have washed their robes and made them white in the blood of the Lamb." The idea here is that the sacrifice of Jesus on the cross has cleansing power.

What stains do you need to hold up to God in confession today? A fresh start and an unblemished record are available through his mercy.

Read: Acts 22:16.
Think: C.S. Lewis said, "When a man is getting better he understands more and more clearly the evil that is still left in him. When a man is getting worse he understands his own badness less and less." Are you getting better at identifying stains that need cleaning?
Pray: Ask God to help you identify and confess moral failure.

DAY 4
THE NÛN AND THE NONES

When the Islamic State swept over Iraq, they marked the homes and businesses of Iraqi Christians with a red nûn. The Arabic letter (pronounced "noon") looks like a "u" with a dot above. It is equivalent to our "N" and stands for "Nazarene," a pejorative Arabic word for those who follow Jesus of Nazareth.

It easily calls to mind the requirement that Jews display the Star of David in Nazi-controlled Germany. The Jewish identifier was a precursor to persecution in twentieth-century Europe, and it's no different with the Christian identifier in twenty-first century Iraq.

Yet Iraqi Christians embraced what was meant as a derogatory mark. Hundreds of thousands around the world followed suit, publicly posting the Arabic "noon" on their social media pages stand in solidarity with their persecuted brothers and sisters.

Reading reports on the "noons" made me think of another label growing in popularity: The Nones.

No, not Catholic nuns. The "Nones" is the label researchers have given to those with no religious affiliation. When asked to identify themselves from a list of religious groups, one of every five now mark the option "None." Among the under-30 Millennials, one of every three do so. That makes the "Nones" the second largest "religious" group in America.

Most Americans were raised in families that were at least nominally Christian. So why do so many now check "None" on a religious survey? One reason is surely our too-human reluctance to identify with a mocked group. We're astute observers of the professor's smirk and the comedian's snark. And we quickly learn that Christian beliefs and morals create severe social and career liabilities. So, when asked to identify our religious affiliation, it's become convenient to shrug and say, "None. I'm spiritual but not religious."

So, in one part of the world people identify with the convenient label "None" while in another part of the world people accept the costly label "Nûn."

What about you? Will you accept the mocked mark? Though Western Christians "have not yet had to resist to the point of being killed" (Hebrews 12:4 GNT), that doesn't mean it won't cost you. But follow the Nazarene who "thought nothing of the disgrace of dying on the cross" (Hebrews 12:3 GNT). He's holding your eternal reward in two nail-scarred hands.

Read: 2 Timothy 2:11-13
Think: What makes you hesitate to openly identify as a Christian?
Pray: Pray for those who face hardship because of their loyalty to Jesus. Pray for God to prepare you to endure such hardship, too.

DAY 5
THE POWER OF YOUR EXPECTATIONS

We all know about the placebo effect, but now researchers are discovering that the "nocebo effect" exists, too. And there's a lesson here about the impact of expectations on our reality.

When testing the effectiveness of a medication, some subjects will be given the real deal while some will be given a placebo, a fake pill. Patients are only told they're in a drug study, and none of them are told whether they're on the trial drug or a placebo. What's interesting is that sometimes the intended outcome of the real medication shows up in those taking the placebo. The simple expectation that the medication will get them better seems to get some patients better. That's what's called the placebo effect.

But now researchers are looking into what has been dubbed the "nocebo effect." When a patient is warned about a medication's potential side effects, sometimes those unwelcome things show up even among the control patients on the placebo. Medically, patients on a fake pill shouldn't suffer any sort of reaction, but the belief that they are on the real medication causes some control patients to suffer the side effects of the real medication. They've reported the nausea, dizziness, impotence, blood-pressure changes, or gastrointestinal pains that they were warned may happen.

Ah, the power of our expectations. And, ah, the power others have over our expectations. Because, you see, researchers of the nocebo effect now caution doctors to be careful in how they communicate the possible effects of their recommended actions. "Words are the most powerful tool a doctor possesses," the renowned cardiologist Bernard Lown once said, "but words, like a two-edged sword, can maim as well as heal."

Now, I don't partake of any poison fruit from the "prosperity theology" tree. But let's acknowledge that our attitudes are powerful things. Either hope or cynicism can have a real impact on whether we make forward progress in life. It can have a real impact on the lives of others, too.

When Jesus stood at the grave of Lazarus (John 11), he told the man's grieving sister, "He who believes in me will live even though he dies." Then he asked an important question: "Do you believe this?"

How you answer that question makes all the difference in how you handle whatever deadness is in your discipleship, your marriage, your grown children, your dreams.

I'm holding out for resurrection.

Do you believe this?

Read: Proverbs 17:22
Think: On a scale of 1-10, how would you rate yourself as a "hopeful" person? How has that attitude impacted your relationship to God and others?
Pray: Ask God to help you hope again.

DAY 6
NO MORE HERMIT HOLES

"God told me it was time to come out of the hole. But I don't know if I have the energy."

I love that line.

It comes from an old Boston Globe story about Thomas Johnson, an eccentric hermit. For ten years he avoided society by wandering deep into a Boy Scout campground on Nantucket Island in Massachusetts and burrowing eight feet underground.

Then a deer hunter stumbled over his stovepipe jutting out of the ground, and soon federal agents and state health officials were demanding he abandon his unauthorized hideaway.

He surrendered to the inevitable. "God told me it was time to come out of the hole," he told the Boston Globe with a shrug, adding, "but I don't know if I have the energy."

Like Thomas Johnson, believers are tempted to burrow down into bunkers in escape from the world around us. But God has told us it's time to come out of our holes. He has told us to go into the world to make disciples (Matthew 28:18-20), to fish for people (Matthew 4:19), and to be preserving salt (Matthew 5:13).

We should always hope that our friends will get to the same point that the Samaritan woman's friends got to in John 4. There we read of a woman's encounter with Jesus at a well. By the end of their conversation, she became convinced that he was the hoped-for Messiah, and ran into town to tell those she knew. After the Samaritans spent 2 days with Jesus, they told the woman, "We no longer believe just because of what you said; now we have heard for ourselves, and we know that this man really is the Savior of the world" (John 4:42).

Isn't that what you hope to hear from your friends?

We all need a fresh reminder to come out of our hermit holes and re-engage with the world for the sake of the good news we have to offer!

Read: Mark 12:28-31
Think: Draw a rough map of your neighborhood or apartment complex. Write in the names of as many neighbors as you can, and a few facts about them. Commit to continue to work on this map as you engage with your neighbors this year.
Pray: Ask God to help you better know and love your neighbors.

DAY 7
AGENTS FOR PEACE
IN A DIVERSE WORLD

When Simon Peter explained the gospel to the religious leaders of his community, he said in Acts 4:12 (GNT), "Salvation is to be found through him alone; in all the world there is no one else whom God has given who can save us." The people he was speaking to didn't like the claim in their day. Not much has changed in our day, either.

In my city, a favorite bumper sticker simply says "COEXIST." The symbols of the world's major religions are used to spell the word. The Muslim crescent moon, for example, becomes the "C," the Star of David serves as the "X," and the cross stands in for the "T."

The decal preaches the conviction that no one religion can corner the market on truth. In fact, many in our culture object to the Christian belief in Jesus as the only way to God. They see it as impolite or even disruptive to the unity of a company or community.

But the gospel message, even with its exclusive claims about Jesus, has the resources to make believers agents for peace. I can think of three resources.

Common Grace: Christianity teaches that there are basic values self-evident to everyone, not just Bible readers. So, we can work together with people of other faiths - and no faith - to build decent communities.

Saving Grace: The gospel teaches that our salvation comes by grace alone. God drew us to himself not because of our nationality or our ethnicity or our moral self-discipline. It wasn't that we were smarter or had a greater moral sensitivity. It's all of grace. So we can relate to others who don't get it, because there was a time when we didn't get it.

The Example of Jesus: At the very heart of the Christian story is a man who died for his enemies, praying for their forgiveness. Reflection on this can only lead to a radically different way of dealing with those who are different from us.

Do Christians always put these resources into practice in their relationships in the world? It's too bad there are enough stories to prove that we don't. But the more we understand the gospel, the more we can communicate the exclusive claims of Jesus in a manner that builds relationships, even with those who don't accept our claims.

Read: Colossians 4:5-6
Think: Play back the last exchange you had with a nonbeliever online or in person. How would the conversation have been better had you remembered the three resources of "common grace," "saving grace," and "the example of Jesus"?
Pray: Ask God to help you live Colossians 4:5-6 today.

DAY 8
A HEARTLESS CRIME

An Irish church had its heart stolen. Let's make sure it doesn't happen to us.

For 900 years Christ Church Cathedral has housed the heart of Dublin's patron saint, Lorcan Ua Tuathail, better known today as Laurence O'Toole. Yes, his literal heart was contained in a wooden box bolted to the wall. But in March 2012 the iron bars surrounding the wooden box were wrenched open and the relic was snatched. Nothing else in the building was taken. Cathedral staff said they were "devastated" at the loss of their heart.

As I said, let's make sure it doesn't happen to us.

We can lose our church's heart, you know. It happened to the ancient Ephesian church. The book of Revelation opens with the risen Christ issuing messages for seven churches. To the Ephesian church Christ gave this warning: "You have forsaken the love you had at first" (Revelation 2:4).

Oh, they were dutiful enough. Jesus began his message to the Ephesians with praise, acknowledging "your deeds, your hard work, and your perseverance." What's more, he congratulated them for guarding Christian truth.

But apparently we can be dutiful and doctrinal -- and dry. When it comes to our actions, we can proceed through the Christian disciplines of prayer and Bible study and tithing as if on autopilot. When it comes to our beliefs, we can protect our Christian convictions more out of unreflective habit than faithfulness.

In other words, we can lose our heart. "I have this against you," Jesus warned the Ephesian believers. "You have forsaken the love you had at first."

If you asked church members what ought to be the church's top priority, some would say, "missions," while others would say, "Bible study." Some would suggest "outreach" or "caring fellowship."

I think Jesus would praise us for these passions, and yet none of these things qualify as the "heart" of our church.

The heart of our church is our love for Jesus. We succeed or fail by the degree of our gratitude for his sacrifice, our obedience to his commands, our prayers for his power, our worship of his worth, and our anticipation of his return.

All of our church's many activities issue from that love, but must never substitute for that love. Ask God to keep you, or return you, to your first love!

> **Read**: Revelation 2:1-7
> **Think**: We need to respond to Christ with both *duty* and *delight*. What consequences follow if we only pay attention to one without the other?
> **Pray**: Ask God to restore the *joy* of your salvation (Psalm 51:12).

DAY 9
DISCOVER HOPE

Botanist Elaine Solowey has successfully grown a palm tree from a seed that's 2,000 years old.

It is the oldest seed ever known to produce a viable young tree, and the news story is a parable about hope.

The seed was discovered decades earlier during archaeological excavations at Masada. When she heard of the excavation's findings, she asked for some of the seeds.

Solowey said she didn't think anything would come of her planting. But then she saw something in the potting soil. "Much to my astonishment, after five weeks, a small little date shoot came up," she said. "It was pale, almost whitish green. The first two leaves were abnormal-looking. They were very flat and very pale. The third leaf started to have the striations of a normal date plant. Now it looks perfectly normal to me." Another researcher at the botanical center said, "It feels remarkable to see this seed growing, to see it coming out of the soil after two thousand years."

The botanist has brought back to life more than 100 rare or near-extinct species of plants and herbs in a study of ancient natural cures, but this is the oldest seed to ever produce new life.

It's not just a story of seeds; it's a story of hope.

Maybe it's been a long time since you've had any of that. If so, you can identify with those downcast disciples in Luke 24. They were walking back to their home in Emmaus after they saw Jesus crucified. Their hope in Jesus's promises had been crushed at the cross.

But then they met Jesus alive, victorious over his horrible death, and hope blossomed.

We've been told that where there's life there's hope, but that's not true. Where there's life there's heartbreak. Where there's life there's unemployment. Where there's life there's Hepatitis C. Where there's life there's divorce.

It's not true that where there's life there's hope. But where there's hope, there's life! As the Canadian musician, Bruce Cockburn, put it:

This world can be better than it is today
You can say I'm a dreamer but that's okay
Without the "Could be" and the "Might have been"
All you've got left is your fragile skin

It's time to discover hope again!

> **Read**: Luke 24:13-35
> **Think**: Who is the most hopeful person you know? How has their confidence impacted their energy, their relationships, and even their attractiveness?
> **Pray**: Ask God to help you live in such a way that someone would list you as the most hopeful person they know.

DAY 10
MEET EL ROI

Do you need a reminder today that God is your *El Roi*?

Of all the titles given to God in the Bible, this one is most insightful. Come to think of it, "insightful" is really the best word here.

In the Bible, we're taught this name for God not by a prophet or a theologian but by a pregnant teenage slave girl named Hagar. When she fled from unfair treatment, God's angel met her in the wilderness and strengthened her. She exclaimed, "I have now seen the One who sees me." From that moment she called the Lord by the name "*El Roi*," which means, "God sees!" (Genesis 16:13).

I wonder if she was drawing from her Egyptian background when she said that. She was raised in a culture that valued cats whose keen eyes enabled them to keep rats out of the dark granaries so essential for life. In fact, the eyes actually glow in the stone idol of the Egyptian goddess Pasht ("Cat") on display in in the Louvre Museum in Paris. The ancient craftsmen highlighted the eyes with some phosphorescent material as a way to emphasize the visual power of their goddess even in the dark. The artwork in the museum is dated a little before the time of Hagar.

It was the Lord that Hagar met in her wilderness experience, not Pasht. But when she described the significance of that meeting, what she valued was God's ability to see her in the darkness of her troubles. So far from home, suffering an intolerable situation, she met a God who said, "I know what you're going through." And she exclaims, "I'm not alone! I have met *El Roi*, the God who sees me!"

The story of God's dealings with Abraham is the main plot of Genesis 12-23, not Hagar. And yet in Genesis 16 there is this gracious side note about God's dealings with his wife's Egyptian handmaiden. And because of that side note, you and I have another "insight" into who God is.

When I'm praying with someone in crisis, one of the phrases I tend to use is, "God, show us in large ways and in a hundred small ways how you are walking with us through this experience." Maybe you need to pray that right now, and then look around for how God is going to answer that prayer. May you see the One who sees you!

Read: Genesis 16:1-16
Think: In what ways does it *comfort* you to think that God sees everything you're going through? In what ways does it *convict* you that God sees everything you're going through?
Pray: Use this prayer request today: "God, show us in large ways and in a hundred small ways how you are walking with us through this experience."

DAY 11
GOD'S FORWARD OBSERVERS

Have you noticed how often the words "watch" and "pray" are combined in the Bible? Our praying should make us more attentive, our attentiveness should lead us more often to prayer, which should make us even more attentive, and on and on in a building cycle.

If we should we watchful, for what should be watching? We should be alert to the activity of God and pray for its success, and we should be alert to the activity of the Evil One and pray for its defeat.

I remember a story from a pastor who was a Vietnam vet. He recounted how his battalion would set up a firebase in the jungle with huge 8-inch guns. Then, companies of soldiers would fan out in four directions from the base, looking for the enemy. Often, when the enemy was found, they would be in much greater number than the company of American soldiers. When that happened, the company would simply get on the radio and call in the coordinates of the enemy so the firebase could rain shells down on them. The vet said that Christians are God's forward observers in enemy territory. And when we encounter the enemy, we must call down the firepower of heaven.

Ever since he visualized prayer in that way for me, it has energized my prayer life. We must be alert to the work of the enemy. We must be sensitive to his ways in personal relationships, church matters, governmental affairs -- we must be awake to his whereabouts, and when we discover his activity, we must radio those coordinates to heaven, calling on the power of divine guns.

We must obey the Scriptures that repeatedly tell us to watch and pray. We must pray for the divine activity we see around us and against the demonic activity we see around us.

How alert are you to these things? Some of us are so focused on our own plans, pains, and pleasures that we have no sensitivity to the spiritual warfare around us. Maybe today you need to confess, "When it comes to my prayer life, I want to be more alert. I've neglected to be God's forward observer. I've been AWOL, but I want to count for him again."

Read: Luke 21:36; 1 Peter 5:8
Think: Identify the ways Satan has sought to make trouble for you, for a loved one, for your church, or in a situation going on in the world.
Pray: Call down the firepower of heaven on this enemy activity.

DAY 12
FOUNDATIONS

Here's a parable for our times: Half of the town of Kiruna, Sweden, is being moved two miles from its current site at a cost of $4 billion. Decades of iron ore mining have slowly eroded the foundations of the town built above the world's largest underground mine.

It's an expensive lesson: Lose the foundation, lose your way of life.

Across the next 40 to 50 years, some buildings will be torn down and rebuilt. Others will be taken down piece by piece and reassembled in their new locale, including a historic wooden church. The church was once voted Sweden's most beautiful building but the ground it was built upon is giving way, so it won't last.

Some remain uncertain that the new location will be any more secure than the sagging earth they're leaving. For the relocation, the state-run mine has chosen a spot where they have deposited waste rock from the mining process.

Nevertheless, most accept the move as inevitable. "The people in Kiruna have known since 100 years ago they were living on iron ore," said Vice Mayor Hans Swedell. "They knew that sometime they would have to move."

As I said: A parable for our times.

A little apathy in our civic duties, chronic laziness in our parenting, a few bad decisions in our business, a few compromises in our church—like the tap, tap, tap of a miner's pick, these things can slowly chip away at the foundations. The consequences aren't immediate, but over time we find we've jeopardized the life we hoped to build.

It's a good reminder for all of us who want to build something that lasts.

In Isaiah 58:12, the prophet looked hopefully for people who would "rebuild the ancient ruins" and "raise up the age-old foundations." Let's be the fulfillment of that prophecy in our own families, churches, community, and nation.

What can you do today to tend the convictions and habits that uphold the things important to you?

Read: Isaiah 58:11-12
Think: What can you do today to tend the convictions and habits that uphold the things important to you?
Pray: Ask God to help you do your part to "rebuild the ancient ruins" and "raise up the age-old foundations" in your family, your church, and your nation.

DAY 13
SWEET TEA FOR THE SOUL

I know a Southernism that can help you develop your soul.

You know what a "Southernism" is, right? People from the South measure distance in "tads" and measure time in "directlys" -- as in "scoot over a tad" and "I'll be over to your house directly." People from the South know that a state of readiness is required to enter into any action, so we'll let you know when we're "fixin'" to do something. And people from the South know that it makes no sense for the plural of "you" to be "you." Every other language differentiates between the second-person singular and the second-person plural, so English should, too. "Y'all" solves the deficiency here. Even my smartphone's autocorrect knows this.

By the way, the best indicator that a speaker has no idea how to imitate a Southerner is when he refers to one person as "y'all." Yankee, please.

But there's one Southernism that will help you develop your soul. I'm speaking about the word "reckon." On his 2012 album, *Punching Bag*, Josh Turner included the song "Whatcha Reckon."

Whatcha reckon we take off early today?
Go and take a little ride in my Chevrolet
Down the road we ain't been down before
And see where it goes

He was inviting his girl to imagine herself in a scenario -- more than that, though: He was inviting her to *act* on the scenario.

And that's where "reckoning" can help you grow as a Christian. In Romans 6:11, Paul says, "Reckon yourselves to be dead indeed to sin, but alive to God in Christ Jesus our Lord" (NKJV).

Is it possible to live a sinful life as a Christian? Of course. We can let the old sinful impulses hold sway. But our challenge is to "reckon" life as otherwise. Paul was saying, "Consider your old sinful life as dead, and live accordingly."

The pursuit of holiness is not a self-improvement process. If you think in these terms, it will lead either to pride or despair, depending on our success. It's better to think of the pursuit of holiness as getting aligned with the status Christ has achieved for us. United to him, we've already died to sin. Spiritual growth means acting in consistency with that scenario.

This great truth is like sweet tea for the soul!

Read: Romans 6:11
Think: Recall your baptism. Picture your old way of life as dead, buried, and gone.
Pray: Ask God to help you live in alignment with that picture.

DAY 14
"WE MUST HAVE THEE, O JESUS OF THE SCARS"

When life hurts, there's nothing like talking with someone who has actually been there. That may be the most powerful distinctive of Christianity among the world's religions. The story of Jesus means that, when it comes to life's hurts, God has been there.

Yale professor Lamin Sanneh was raised Muslim but was drawn to Christ through reflecting on the very thing that Muslims believe did not happen to Christ: the crucifixion. The Qur'an teaches that God spared Jesus from the agony of the cross and 'somebody else' was put in Jesus' place (4:155). For the book, *Finding God at Harvard*, Sanneh writes:

> As hard as I tried, I could not run from the question, 'Who died on the cross?' If we don't know his name, how can we know the God who put him there? But suppose Jesus did die on the cross, and suppose God intended it to be so; how would that change our knowledge of God? I reflected on the suffering and the heartbreak which are part of life, hopes that are often dashed to pieces.... It seemed to me that deep down at the center and core of life, the cross and its anonymous burden was declaring something about

the inner integrity and mystery of life which rang true to all authentic experience....God actually did demonstrate his solidarity with humanity by visibly entering our world and defeating death itself.

Likewise, it was Christ's sufferings that restored Edward Shillito's faith after experiencing the horrors of the First World War. Reflecting on the moment when the risen Jesus shows the scars of his crucifixion to his disciples (John 20:19-29), Shillito wrote:

If we have never sought, we seek Thee now;
Thine eyes burn through the dark, our only stars;
We must have sight of thorn-pricks on Thy brow;
We must have Thee, O Jesus of the Scars.

The heavens frighten us; they are too calm;
In all the universe we have no place.
Our wounds are hurting us; where is the balm?
Lord Jesus, by Thy Scars we claim Thy grace....

The other gods were strong, but Thou wast weak;
They rode, but Thou didst stumble to a throne;
But to our wounds only God's wounds can speak,
And not a god has wounds, but Thou alone.

If life hurts right now, trust in the One who endured life's hurts and triumphed!

Read: John 20:19-29
Think: Whatever you're facing right now, reflect on how Jesus experienced the same thing.
Pray: Ask God to help you trust in the One who endured life's hurts and triumphed.

DAY 15
WHO GOD SAYS YOU ARE

When it comes to the names we're given, I'm glad God puts more thought into it than some parents.

John Tierney once ran a contest for bad baby names. He got more than 1,000 entries of real names. There was Charman Toilette, Chastity Beltz, Wrigley Fields, Justin Credible, Candy Stohr, and Tiny Bimbo. I suppose Brook Traut had good reason to name his daughter Rainbow, but the dad who named his daughter Emma Royd should be shot.

The winner of the contest? Well, how to put this? Iona is a pretty name, but the mother really didn't think about how it would sound when paired with the family name -- Knipl. Before taking her husband's name, she said that every time she introduced herself the typical reply was, "I own two."

I'm reminded of a scene from the 70s sitcom, *WKRP in Cincinnati*. (Yes, I really am that old.) Les Nessman was a slight, balding, bespectacled newsman for the radio station. When he met a young, handsome repairman, the exchange went like this:

Nessman: Steel, is it?

Hawthorne: Yeah, Steel Hawthorn.

Nessman: That's a nice name.

Hawthorne: Thanks. I like to think that a person's name says a lot about the type of person he is. What was your name again?

Nessman: [pauses] Les.

Parents may give their kids a name they have to live down, but God gives us titles to live up to! Have you ever thought about the ways God has named you? For a start, how about . . .

. . . Overcomer (1 John 5:4)

. . . Holy (Colossians 1:22)

. . . Free (John 8:36)

Do we live up to these titles? Not yet, not always. But God calls you up to and in to the character he knows you can become.

Let's think through what it means to live under God's inspiring labels.

Read: Judges 6:1-12. Pay attention to the title the angel gave Gideon and whether he deserved that title at that stage in his life.
Think: What is your favorite title that God has assigned to his people?
Pray: Ask God to help you live up to the character he knows you can become.

DAY 16
WHO'S ON YOUR FRIDGE?

"Can I take your picture?" Peter Bregman asked. "I want you on my fridge."

Bregman was talking with Marvin, a man in his 70s, working out with boxing gloves in the gym. Bregman knew little about him, having just met him. But the man's energy and sunny outlook were an inspiration. So he took his picture.

Which sparked a thought: Why not start a collection? "A collection of pictures of ordinary people, about whom I know very little, but who inspire me with some quality I want to nurture in myself." He wrote about it for Fast Company magazine.

What a great idea! If your fridge displayed little snapshots of ordinary people who inspired you, whose photos would you post?

The practice wouldn't just help us in our personal development. It would also change what we decide to look for in others. Bregman writes:

> We focus on what people are doing wrong, on their weaknesses and shortcomings. We gossip and complain. We get frustrated

and passive aggressive. We find ourselves constantly surprised by the flaws of our colleagues: How could he/she/they do that?

What if, instead -- or at least in addition -- we chose not to miss an opportunity to be inspired? If we gossiped about things people did that energized us without fixating on the things that disappointed us? If we looked for sparks that ignited our enthusiasm and incited our goodwill? And if we allowed those sparks to light our fires of passion?

Believers, of all people, should be good at finding inspiring qualities in others. The Bible informs us that every person is made in the image of God. Yes, we are all fallen image-bearers who reveal our fallenness at every turn. And yet everyone still has what Pascal called "rumors of glory." As Aslan told the children in Narnia, "You come from the Lord Adam and the Lady Eve. And that is honor enough to erect the head of the poorest beggar, and shame enough to bow the shoulders of the greatest emperor on earth."

Shame and honor. Both. At the same time.

We should never forget the great capacity that fallen people have to disappoint -- and plan accordingly. And yet we should never forget whose image fallen people still bear -- and catch our breath when we see it.

And, maybe, preserve the moment in a snapshot for our fridge.

Read: Psalm 119
Think: If you followed Peter Bregman's practice, whose picture would you put on your fridge, and why?
Pray: Ask God to help you spend this day identifying whatever is admirable and inspiring in the people around you.

DAY 17
BENCHMARKS OF SPIRITUAL GROWTH

Some of the most significant Bible verses are at the third chapter and sixteenth verse of a Bible book. Have you ever noticed this?

I'm not saying there's anything mystical about this. It's just an intriguing point.

John 3:16 is probably the most famous scripture reference. It has appeared on banners and overpasses. It's been printed on shopping bags from Forever 21 and cups from In-N-Out Burger. Back in 2009 Tim Tebow led the Florida Gators to the national college football championship over the Oklahoma Sooners wearing the scripture reference on his eyeblack. Under one eye was the word "John" and under the other eye were the numbers "3:16." During that game, 94 million people went online and entered the search term "John 3:16." Read it and you learn the message we should embrace and then share with others: "For God so loved the world that he gave his one and only Son, that whoever believes in him shall not perish but have eternal life."

But then there are other important passages at the third chapter and sixteenth verse of a New Testament book. Read Colossians 3:16 and you learn the importance of worship: "Let the message of Christ dwell among you richly as you teach and admonish one another with all wisdom through psalms, hymns, and songs from the Spirit, singing to God with gratitude in your hearts."

Read 1 John 3:16 and you discover the nature of Christian fellowship: "Jesus Christ laid down his life for us. And we ought to lay down our lives for our brothers and sisters."

Read 2 Timothy 3:16 and you find out why Bible study is so important: "All Scripture is God-breathed and is useful for teaching, rebuking, correcting and training in righteousness."

Some creative person could probably create a discipleship course based upon the "3:16" passages. It's all there. The disciple's task is to worship and pray to God (Colossians 3:16), study his Word (2 Timothy 3:16), fellowship with other believers (1 John 3:16), and share the message of salvation with others (John 3:16).

Before this 40-day project is up, take a moment to measure yourself against these four benchmarks of spiritual growth. No matter how far you've advanced in the faith, the goals Christ wants you to pursue haven't changed.

Read: Acts 2:42
Think: Which of the four "3:16" activities in today's devotional is your strongest practice? Which is your weakest?
Pray: Ask God to help you review your spiritual growth against these four "3:16" practices and to plan for personal improvement.

DAY 18
OBJECTS IN MIRROR ARE CLOSER THAN THEY APPEAR

"Surely the Lord is in this place, and I was not aware of it!"

Most of us have made that astonished confession at least once. For Jacob, the realization came during a crisis.

Jacob was a young single adult who had never thought much about God. He heard the stories of how father Isaac and grandfather Abraham met the Lord, but God was irrelevant to his life. It wasn't that he had considered God and rejected him. No, he had never really considered God. He wasn't an atheist: he had simply never seen the relevance on his life of God's existence. But then he met the Lord that his father and grandfather had talked about, and he exclaimed, "Surely the Lord is in this place, and I was not aware of it!" (Genesis 28:16)

Maybe that needs to be your confession:

"The Lord is in my home, and I was not aware of it!"

"The Lord is in my diagnosis, and I was not aware of it!"

"The Lord is at work in my city, and up to this point I've written it off as a place to suffer through and escape."

"The Lord is in my rebellion, and I was not aware of it!"

In verse 17 he says, "How awesome is this place! This is none other than the house of God; this is the gate of heaven." What a contrast to verse 11, where this location is simply called "a certain place," and we're told that Jacob lay down there for no other reason than that the sun had set. But now he says, "This is more than just a certain old place. This is an awesome place! God is all around! This is the point where earth and heaven intersect!"

My car's side mirror warns, "Objects in mirror are closer than they appear." God really is closer than you think. In the mid-19th century Frederick Hosmer wrote:

O Thou, in all Thy might so far,
In all Thy love so near,
Beyond the range of sun and star,
And yet beside us here.

We all need a fresh reminder that God is involved in our lives. Be on the lookout for his activity in your life today.

Read: Genesis 28:1-16
Think: Recall a time that God reminded you of his presence when you needed it most.
Pray: Ask God to reveal his presence in your current circumstances.

DAY 19
THE MOST IMPORTANT WORD YOU'LL LEARN THIS WEEK

Maybe you read about the South Korean woman who was granted her driver's license after 960 tries. Her tenacity has given new meaning to a popular Korean term: *sajeonogi*.

It's the most important word you'll learn this week. But first, the driver's license story.

The New York Times wrote about Cha Sa-soon, a 69-year-old widow who lives in a remote village in South Korea. She wanted to learn to drive so she could take her grandkids to the zoo without relying on the bus system. But Ms. Cha had limited reading skills, having begun school at 15 only to drop out for lack of funds a few years later. So, her biggest obstacle was the 50-minute written test consisting of 40 multiple-choice questions. She failed this exam 959 times, at a cost of $5 for each try.

But she never gave up, and she's the proud owner of a driver's license today. She's also the proud owner of a $17,000 car from the people of Hyundai, who featured her on prime-time commercials in Korea.

The New York Times piece says she's become the embodiment of *sajeonogi*.

That's a conflation of four words that capture a proverb on perseverance:

Sa means "four"
Jeon means "to be knocked down"
Oh means "five"
Gi means "to rise"

So, *sajeonogi* means, "Rise five times when knocked down four times." The idiom became popular after Korean boxer Hong-Su-hwan won the 1977 super bantamweight championship by a knockout after being floored four times.

No one makes an impact without perseverance. Think of Paul the Apostle. As you read about his first missionary journey in Acts 13-14, he faced many setbacks. A co-worker abandoned him, his health broke down, and he met with hot opposition. Still, he never gave up, and so "the word of the Lord spread through the whole region" (13:49).

Maybe life has knocked you down recently. The really important question, though, is why you're still on the floor. Beat the count, rise up, and get back in there.

Read: Galatians 6:9
Think: What have you recently quit that you need to start up again?
Pray: Ask God to give you *sajeonogi*.

DAY 20
TO FORBEAR IS DIVINE

When giving guidance on life with others, Paul said we should be busy—as the old King James Version puts it—"forbearing one another and forgiving one another." (Colossians 3:13)

Between the two, you're going to have to forbear a lot more than you'll have to forgive.

Think about it. If you forgive your marriage partner for adultery, that may become the subject of a magazine article. But you may never have to struggle to forgive something like that. Instead, you are much more likely required to forbear your husband's irritating habit of using the remote to switch between three shows at a time!

Across my years, I've heard a lot of sermons on forgiveness, I've read a lot of books on forgiveness, and I've been inspired by a lot of dramatic stories about forgiveness. But it's forbearance that is demanded of us a lot more often.

How can you increase your capacity for forbearance? Pay attention to four things.

Personality. Some are introverts, others are extroverts. In making decisions, some are rational and others are spontaneous. Not everyone thinks like us, reacts like us, or communicates like us. The more we know this, the better we can forbear.

Perspective. As the old saying goes, "Don't judge a man until you've walked a mile in his shoes." The old proverb advises us to see things as others see them. In that way, we become more understanding of others.

Progress. We can be more patient with people if we take into account where they are in their physical and emotional and spiritual progress. For example, some of us who are parents of small children have to admit we get so impatient with our kids because we don't take into account what an ordeal it is to tie shoes or get the zipper on the jacket started. If we'll keep in mind that people are at different stages than we are physically, emotionally, and spiritually, it will help us bear irritations in relationships.

Problems. Someone else's behavior may spring from the stuff they're dealing with: their parents' divorce, their husband's Alzheimer's, their adult child's poor choices, their shame, their fears, their regrets. The more we know that and the more we take it into account, the more we can bear with other people.

Forgiveness is more dramatic, but forbearance is more *daily*. Be prepared to exercise a little forbearance today.

Read: Colossians 3:13
Think: List the things you have to "forebear" in others. List things they probably have to "forebear" in you.
Pray: Ask God to help you forebear another person by giving you sensitivity to his or her *personality*, *perspective*, *progress*, and *problems*.

DAY 21
DON'T LOOK BACK

In his book, *Onward*, Russell Moore wrote about the long adoption process he and his wife went through. Finally the time came for them to travel to Moscow and receive their new sons. But at first the boys were far from joyful at leaving the horrific Russian orphanage. "They'd never seen the sun, and they'd never felt the wind. They had never heard the sound of a car door slamming or had the sensation of being carried along at 100 miles an hour down a road. I noticed that they were shaking, and reaching back to the orphanage in the distance."

Their new father whispered them, "That place is a pit! If only you knew what's waiting for you: a home with a Mommy and a Daddy who love you, grandparents and great-grandparents and cousins and playmates and McDonald's Happy Meals!"

But all they knew was the orphanage. It was squalid, but it was familiar. They had known no other home. Since then, of course, the boys have become thoroughly acclimated to their new home and country. "I still remember, though, those little hands reaching for the orphanage." Moore writes.

That image should haunt us. After all, the Bible often reminds us that we are sons and daughters of God by adoption. It should completely change how we view things, but sometimes it doesn't. "We get too comfortable with this orphanage universe," Moore writes, "We're content with the world we know."

Have your hands been "reaching back for the orphanage"? Are you looking back longingly at things you should joyfully abandon for Christ's sake?

When Paul wrote the Corinthian believers, he warned them against pining for their old way of life (1 Corinthians 10:1-22). They were to leave it behind and move forward with God. But it's hard to walk forward if you're keeping one foot in the past.

It took years of an adoptive father's patient reassurance before Moore's sons quit pining for their past. Be grateful for your heavenly Father's patience as he waits for our hearts to slowly turn toward the life he wants us living. In Hosea 11:4, God said,

> I led them with cords of human kindness,
>   with ties of love.
> To them I was like one who lifts
>   a little child to the cheek,
>   and I bent down to feed them.

Trust that this God wants what's best for you, and turn your face toward him.

Read: 1 Corinthians 10:13
Think: What has God freed you from and yet you still find yourself pining for it?
Pray: Ask God to show you the way out he has provided for your current temptation.

DAY 22
FIT YOUR STORY INTO GOD'S BIGGER STORY

Your faith gets tested when the doctor's report isn't what you had hoped, or when you're laid flat by unexpected cruelty, or a tragedy turns your world upside down. The only way to make sense of life's pain is to fit your story into the Bigger Story that we find in the Bible.

The Bigger Story consists of three "acts."

Creation. After God created our world, he didn't say "oops" (Genesis 1). But when sin entered the picture, it fundamentally altered God's good world. Now "the whole creation has been groaning as in the pains of childbirth" under its "bondage to decay" (Romans 8). So, we're going to experience the broken heart of life in a broken world. In fact, the more we see life from this perspective, the more we'll see any moments of joy as mercies and not rights (Psalm 145:9). And God has been so merciful!

Cross. Of all the world's religions, only one describes God as experiencing the ruin of the world as a man. In *The Cross of Christ* John Stott wrote, "I could never myself believe in God, if it were not for the cross. In the real world of pain, how could one worship a God who was immune to it?" That means that whenever I pray about my problems, I'm praying to One who can say, "I know what you're talking about." But on the cross he was doing more than just identifying with the ruin of the world: He was carrying away the sin that ruined the world. That's why to me the most beautiful line in *The Passion of the Christ* was Jesus to Mary as he stumbled under the weight of the cross he carried: "See, Mother, I make all things new."

Crown. By carrying away the sin of the ruined the world, Jesus ensured a rescue that will be completed at his glorious return. As the Bible says (Hebrews 2), "at present we do not see everything subject to him" -- but that's only "at present." Just as D-Day was the decisive act of World War 2 that assured the eventual victory in Europe, Christ's death and resurrection was the beginning of the end. We wait in hope for that end, assured that "our present sufferings are not worth comparing with the glory that will be revealed in us" at Christ's return (Romans 8).

All our little stories only make sense in this Bigger Story. "Therefore encourage each other with these words" (1 Thessalonians 4:18).

Read: Romans 8:18-25
Think: Practice telling the Bigger Story provided in this devotional so you will be ready to share it with another person without notes.
Pray: Ask God to help you share this Bigger Story with another person.

DAY 23
GOOD RIDDANCE DAY

In New York, a business group and the city's sanitation department invited residents to dispose of their bad memories. They set up shredders in the Times Square Visitors Center and declared it "Good Riddance Day."

They accepted anything and everything. Photos of ex-lovers. Lousy report cards. Loathed CDs. The organizers even provided a form for people to jot down memories they wished would go away, and then they could shred those forms.

A grand prize of $250 was awarded to the one most creative in letting go of old baggage.

The Apostle Paul could have won an award like that. In Philippians 3:12-14, he told us that the only way to advance in spiritual maturity is to shred the past:

> I press on to take hold of that for which Christ Jesus took hold of me. Brothers, I do not consider myself yet to have taken hold of it. But one thing I do: Forgetting what is behind and straining toward what is ahead, I press on toward the goal to win the prize for which God has called me heavenward in Christ Jesus.

Now, Paul was not saying that there was more he had to do to win God's approval. Our relationship to God is based on what he did for us, not what we do for him. Because of the cross of Christ, God gives you his gift of eternal life. There is nothing incomplete about that.

But Jesus has not only done a work *for* you that's finished; he is also doing a work *in* you that's unfinished. He wants to bring you up ever higher in Christian maturity.

And for that, you'll need to toss out some things.

First, forget the failures that have paralyzed you with guilt. Some of us have slowed to a crawl in the race to Christian maturity because we're dragging this mighty weight of guilt behind us every step of the way. Why do we still carry what our Savior has carried away?

But we need to forget not only our mistakes but also our successes. Believe it or not, success is as potent as guilt in slowing us down. Have you ever noticed that you can't run and pat yourself on the back at the same time? That's true metaphorically as well as literally!

Life's journey involves "forgetting what is behind" and then "straining toward what is ahead." So, let today be "Good Riddance Day" for you!

Read: Philippians 3:12-14
Think: What do you need to mentally shred to make today your Good Riddance Day?
Pray: Ask God to help you press on toward the goal to win the prize for which God has called you heavenward in Christ Jesus.

DAY 24
YOUR WORK MATTERS TO GOD

Maybe you bowed your head for a quick word of thanks over your bowl of cereal this morning. But have you ever thought of all the people God employed to get those flakes on your spoon?

He used farmers to plant and cultivate. He used employees at companies that supply the equipment farmers need, and bankers who arranged the financing for these businesses. He used scientists who check the food for purity. He used plant operators who processed the grain into crispy flakes. He used manufacturers of the trucks that get the boxed-up cereal to market, and the truckers who drive, and the truck stop operators who make their routes possible. He used the engineers who designed the highway, and the laborers who laid down all those miles of road work. He even used the humble pallet makers who hammered together sturdy wood strips to make it easier for the fork lift drivers (whom God also used) to unload the boxes of cereal at the delivery dock of your grocery store. And then there's the high school student who stocked the shelves and the clerk who scanned your selection at check out.

God used a lot of people to get breakfast to your table this morning.

Your work, too, is a vital part of this vast, complex system God directs to meet the needs of this world. Because of that, God is as interested in the quality of your work as he is the quality of your prayers. Life in God's kingdom is more than a daily quiet time and weekend attendance at a church service. Life in God's kingdom also means drilling supply wells, debugging code, administering medicine, keeping a building clean and sanitary, teaching math . . . .

Well, you get the picture.

In 1 Thessalonians 4:11 Paul wrote, "Make it your ambition to lead a quiet life, to mind your own business and to work with your hands, just as we told you, so that your daily life may win the respect of outsiders and so that you will not be dependent on anybody."

I love how Paul combined the phrases "make it your ambition" and "to lead a quiet life" in that text. To our minds, the words don't belong together, but the Apostle regarded them as a perfect match. "Be driven by this passion," he said. What passion? "Be ambitious to settle down into stable self-sustaining labor."

Your work matters to God. If you're employed, thank him for work to go to. And then go out and do it well as part of your obedience to God.

Read: 1 Thessalonians 4:11
Think: How is God using your work to meet human needs?
Pray: Ask God to help you glorify him in the way you do your work today.

DAY 25
TEACH US TO NUMBER OUR DAYS

There's a new wrist watch that will calculate when you're likely to die and then display that date on the dial. The creators say they designed it "to remind you to make most of your life, and most importantly, to be happy."

It's called Tikker. Get it?

Just send $59 along with a questionnaire about your health habits, risk factors, and age, and a Tikker can be customized to your demise.

"It's not an entirely bizarre idea," wrote Olga Khazan, who reported on the device for The Atlantic. "We tend to value things that are scarce, and death is, after all, a scarcity of life. Thinking about death can make us appreciate life more, and it can also make us into better people."

Actually, there's some truth there. According to a study reported in Fast Company, thinking about money makes you less ethical while thinking about time makes you more ethical. Researchers surmise it has to do with considering your limited time and how you'll be regarded as you leave this earth.

Maybe that's why Moses didn't ask God, "Teach us to number our dollars" but rather, "Teach us to number our days" (Psalm 90:12).

Of course, Moses wasn't asking to know the day of his death (sorry, Tikker). Instead, he was wanting God's help so that the fact of his death would sink in.

Depressing? Moses didn't think so. Instead, his prayer to God means he recognized his desperate need of such information.

You need that information, too.

The most sobering thing I've ever done was to write my own eulogy. For a college class, I was assigned to write a summary of my life. It had a remarkable clarifying effect at the age of 19 to write about myself in the past tense—and then to put a period at the end of the last sentence describing my life.

Of course, the eulogy was nothing more than a thought experiment. And the future date on the Tikker is nothing more than an actuarial guess.

In other words, the date of your death cannot be known. The fact of it, though? That's what needs to settle deep into our souls. And only then can we start the hard work of clarifying our priorities and aligning our choices accordingly.

Let's get to that good work. Tick tock, people.

Read: Psalm 90
Think: If you had a month left to live, what would you do differently?
Pray: Ask God to teach you to number your days that you may gain a heart of wisdom (Psalm 90:12).

DAY 26
LONGING FOR LIGHT

The 198 residents of Bondo, Switzerland want sunlight, and they're planning to build a giant mirror to catch it.

According to an Associated Press story, Bondo lies so deep in the Bregaglia Valley that residents are deprived of sunlight between December and February. So, they are planning to build a $130,000 mirror to reflect sunlight down into their valley.

It's been done before. The Italian town of Viganella installed a 26-by-16 feet sheet of reflective steel to direct sunlight to their homes at the bottom of a steep Alpine valley.

People long for light, and Christ expects his followers to shine in a dark world. Jesus said, "You are the light of the world—like a city on a hilltop that cannot be hidden" (Matthew 5:14, NLT). The way we live, the convictions we hold, the forgiveness we show, the discipline we maintain, the generosity we display—it all serves as a light that brightly displays God's truth.

In West Virginia folklore there's a tale about a couple who called for a doctor late one night as the wife was ready to deliver a baby. The country physician turned the rustic farmhouse into a makeshift delivery room. The husband was handed a lantern and instructed to hold it up so the doctor could see. After a healthy boy was born the man lowered the lantern. The doctor shouted for this new father to get the lantern up as he delivered another baby—this time a girl. The father was thrown into shock when the doctor once again insisted that the light be held up. He said, "We can't stop now, it looks like there's another one."

The shaky father then asked the doctor, "Do you think it's the light that's attracting 'em?"

Actually, I'd say the hillbilly was on to something. As we put Christ's teaching into practice, it illuminates the path for others. And those who have grown tired of a life without light will find that incredibly attractive. So, hold the light up today.

Read: Matthew 5:14
Think: Recall a time when you had to fumble in the dark (for example, on a camping trip, or after a power outage). What did you find limiting or unsettling about the experience? How is your witness like "light" to others?
Pray: Ask God to help your witness be a light to those who do not yet know God.

DAY 27
A BROKEN WORLD AND A GOOD GOD

Have you had a "but even so" moment yet?

Kobayashi Issa was an 18th century haiku master. In my favorite of his poems he wrote:

The world of dew is, yes,
a world of dew,
but even so

As a lay Buddhist priest, Issa believed that the best response to suffering was stoic detachment, freeing oneself from the impulse to cling possessively to impermanent things. In his haiku, then, he acknowledged the way he was taught to see the world -- as ephemeral dew. And yet with that last line he pushed back against this worldview at the same time.

Given his experience with suffering, the pushback is understandable. As Pico Iyer wrote in the New York Times:

Issa had seen his mother die when he was 2, his first son die, his father contract typhoid fever, his next son and a beloved daughter die. He knew that suffering was a fact of life, he might have been saying in his short verse; he knew that impermanence is our home and loss the law of the world. But how could he not wish, when his 1-year-old daughter contracted smallpox, and expired, that it be otherwise?

No matter how neatly we arrange our worldview, suffering scrambles it. This is true whether we're founding life on Buddhist principles or secular sensibilities or Christian convictions.

What does the Christian do with her belief in an all-powerful, all-loving God when heartbreak crashes in? This may be one of the toughest challenges to our faith. It's certainly the most personal.

I read a fascinating report in Wired about a study in pain management. In experiments, scientists found that we survive pain better if our minds are occupied with thoughts of someone we love.

Exactly so. In the Christian worldview, we process suffering by focusing on the One who suffered for us. Of all the world's religions, only one describes God as experiencing the ruin of the world as a man. But on the cross he was doing more than just identifying with the ruin of the world: He was carrying away the sin that ruined the world so that he could begin the process of making all things new.

Are you in pain? Focus on the Beloved and see how well that can get you through.

Read: Hebrews 4:14-16
Think: Scientists have found that we survive pain better if our minds are occupied with thoughts of someone we deeply love. Why do you think this is so?
Pray: Approach God's throne of grace with confidence, so that you may receive mercy and find grace to help you in your time of need.

DAY 28
ARE YOU AFRAID TO WIN?

I know perfectionists driven by a fear of failure, but I've seen more people crippled by the fear of success.

Fear of success? Who could possibly be afraid of success? Could the answer be... you?

Eugene Peterson recalled a time when he was five years old, standing at a barbed-wire fence, watching a neighbor named "Brother Storm." The man rumbled up and down the field in his enormous tractor, and the daily wish of little Peterson was to ride on that John Deere.

One day while the little preschooler stood by the fence with that mixture of awe and longing, Brother Storm stopped. He stood up from the seat, and made strong waving motions to Peterson with his arm. "He looked mean and angry," said Peterson. "I knew I was probably where I shouldn't be; five-year-old boys often are. I turned and left. Sadly, I hadn't felt I was doing anything wrong -- I was only watching from what I thought was a safe distance and wishing that someday, somehow I could get to ride that tractor. I went home feeling rejected, rebuked."

The next Sunday at church, Brother Storm approached young Peterson. "Why didn't you accept my invitation the other day? I was hoping you'd ride with me a while." In his preschool eyes, Peterson thought the man was shooing him away when instead he was beckoning him into an experience the little boy had long desired.

I wonder how many times God calls us into what we most want to do, but we think he's shooing us away.

We fear success. We fear the work success requires, we fear the ridicule our dreams might bring from others, and we desperately fear that we might not have what it takes. After all, if there was no possibility of failure, they'd call it "sure-thing-taking," not "risk-taking!"

Every venture is a test of our mettle, and some of us would rather stay within the safe confines of our private dreams instead of face the risks.

Those of us most crippled by the fear of success are most surprised by Psalm 20. "May he give you the desire of you heart," the poet prays for the king, "and make all your plans succeed." Imagine that: God put that prayer in his Book so we would have permission to talk to him about our desires!

Are you hiding your timidity behind pious-sounding excuses? Trust God with your dreams!

Read: Psalm 20
Think: What do you hope to accomplish before your life is through?
Pray: Since God already knows your ambitions anyway, talk to him about them in prayer. Ask him to help you accomplish your dreams, or to be at peace with other plans God may have for you.

DAY 29
WHY YOU EXIST

Does life have any purpose? If so, what is it?

In his award-winning entry, "Repetition," spoken-word poet Phil Kaye said:

My mother taught me this trick, If you repeat something over and over again, it loses its meaning....Our existence, she said, is the same way. You watch the sunset too often, and it just becomes 6pm. You make the same mistake over and over, you'll stop calling it a mistake. If you just wake up, wake up, wake up, wake up, wake up, wake up, wake up one day you'll forget why.

Have you forgotten why?

I suggest a single word for the purpose of life.

Love.

To discover you are loved by the Creator. To trust that everything you experience is filtered through his loving intentions. To gladly respond to his commands knowing that they are for your good. To enjoy his creation in accordance with his instructions. To relate to men and women around you as those God also cherishes. Love is the purpose of life.

Peggy Noonan once wrote:

We're locked in a funny arc, most of us, in terms of what we know. When you are goony and fourteen years old you think the most important thing in life is love. Then you mature, become more sober and thoughtful, and realize the most important thing in life is achieving, leaving your mark - making breakthroughs in the field of science, or winning an Academy Award in recognition of a serious body of work, or creating security for yourself and your family through having a good house and sending your kids to good schools. And then you get old and realize...the most important thing in life is love. Giving love to others and receiving it from God. All the rest, the sober thoughtful things, are good and constructive...but love is the thing. The rest is just more or less what you were doing between fourteen and wisdom (*Simply Speaking*, pages 53-54).

Love is the reason there is something and not nothing. Live out of this truth at the center, and it changes everything.

Read: 1 John 4:8
Think: Do you think Peggy Noonan's observation is a good summary of the purpose of life?
Pray: Ask God to help you live out of this truth at the center.

DAY 30
PROOF OF LIFE

How would you convince someone you're alive? It took a Romanian man a year of expensive litigation, and as I read his story it made me think about our life in Christ.

When Gheroghe Stirbu tried to renew his identity card, Romanian officials told him that he was dead. Chalk another one up to government bureaucracy: Stirbu had been confused with another man. It took a year for the government to acknowledge their mistake -- and then they charged him for the court costs! "I will of course appeal the imposition of the costs," Mr. Stirbu said, "but I am already beginning to wonder whether or not I would have been better off staying dead."

When I baptize someone I recite a paraphrase of Romans 6:4. I say, "You are buried with Christ in baptism and raised to walk in a new way of life." The problem is, sometimes we find ourselves in a position like Mr. Stirbu: Our "aliveness" is up for question.

Maybe certain habits that should have been left behind still occupy our hearts and routines.

Maybe sour attitudes still flow like poison through our veins.

Maybe we can't seem to find enthusiasm for connecting with other believers for prayer and support.

Maybe, given the choice between reading God's word or a night of idle web surfing, the mouse wins.

Maybe we can't remember the last time we shared the gospel with someone.

What proof could you offer that you are alive in Christ?

Don't get me wrong. No amount of behavior modification or attitude adjustment will set you right with God. It's the other way around. Entering into God's grace results in a new way of life. If we have little evidence that we're alive in Christ, the first thing we have to do is reflect on God's amazing grace to us. Every change and every commitment we make after that is just our "thank you" to God.

Find a way to express that gratitude to God today and show someone you're alive in him!

Read: Romans 6:1-4
Think: How is this guidance from this passage similar to other plans for self-improvement? How is it different?
Pray: Ask God to help you display "proof of life" today.

DAY 31
SAINTS ALIVE!

Pope Francis made headlines when he made saints of two former popes. The media didn't make as much fuss when I was declared a saint.

What? You didn't know that I'm a saint?

There are at least three ways people misunderstand the word. First, many think the word describes someone who has matured spiritually to a point above ordinary people. "She's a saint," we say about the woman who exhibits extraordinary grace under extraordinary pressure.

Second, some think "saint" is just another word for "sanctimonious." It conjures up images like Dana Carvey's "Church Lady" character from re-runs of Saturday Night Live. In Carvey's skits, the Church Lady would draw her lips into a disapproving pucker and sarcastically say, "Well, isn't that special?" as she began her rant against behavior she disliked.

Third, some think of a saint as a hermit in a desert lodge removed from the realities of daily life. With the responsibilities of daily living, who's got time to be a saint?

Because of these misunderstandings, believers hesitate to call themselves "saints." In reality, though, "saint" is a common title for common believers.

As you read Paul's letters, for example, notice how he addressed the believers with the phrase, "To the saints who are in Ephesus" (Ephesians 1:1), or "To all the saints in Christ Jesus who are at Philippi" (Philippians 1:1). The word "saints" is found about forty-five times in the New Testament as a title for God's people, and it shows up another twenty-three times in the Old Testament, primarily in the Psalms. The word "saint" is a translation of the Greek word *hagios*, which means "holy one."

So, believer, you're a saint. What should you do about that?

First, praise God for the status. Your status as a "holy one" is based on what God has done for you, not what you have done for God. So, thank him for the cleansing work of the cross!

Second, live up to the status. God declares us "holy ones" by the work of the cross and sets out to make us "holy ones" by the work of the Spirit. Let him mold you into someone more patient, more faithful, more disciplined, more sensitive to others' needs.

The media hasn't caught up with the news that you're a saint. No worries. I've got it on good authority that the angels rejoice (Luke 15:7, 10).

Read: Ephesians 4:11-13
Think: Do you hesitate to own the word "saint" because you don't want the responsibility that comes with that title?
Pray: Praise God for the status of "holy one" that he has given you through the work of Christ, and ask for his help living up to that status through the work of the Spirit.

DAY 32
A CRIPPLE AT THE KING'S TABLE

You can find "me" in "Mephibosheth." In the name, of course, but also in the story.

Mephibosheth was the son of Jonathan, the closest friend of our beloved Old Testament character, David. Jonathan loved David as deeply as his father, King Saul, hated David. Jonathan loved David despite the fact that David would be king instead of him. David indeed became king upon Saul's death in battle -- in a battle that took Jonathan's life, too.

It was a few years into his reign that David found Jonathan's last remaining son, Mephibosheth. The young man was crippled in both feet from an accident in infancy. In fact, he probably received his name on the same day he received his injury: On the day his father fell in battle and his household ran for their lives. You see, his nickname means, "He who scatters shame." When David found him, "Shame-spreader" was living in Lo Debar which roughly translates as "Nowhere."

He was a real nowhere man, living in a nowhere land.

It was common for new kings to rid themselves of anyone connected to a former monarchy. But David called Mephibosheth into his presence and extended remarkable love to him for the sake of Jonathan. He ordered Jonathan's family estate to be returned to the crippled exile. He assigned servants to work the land so Mephibosheth would have a livable income. And -- here's the most beautiful part -- David said, "You will always eat at my table."

As I said, you can find "me" in "Mephibosheth," because his story is my story. God searched me out and found me. And though I was handicapped by sin and living in Nowhere-land, yet he loved me for the sake of someone else. For the sake of Jesus, he promised me, "You will always eat at my table." And so here I am, blessed beyond all expectation, a cripple at the King's Table.

Do you see your relationship to God on these terms? Everything about the Christian life springs from this awareness. In the New Testament, over and over again when we're told to live a certain way or maintain a certain attitude or make a certain choice, we're always told to do so in light of God's grace to the undeserving. So, live out of the humble gratitude that comes from seeing Christianity in these terms.

Read: 2 Samuel 9:1-13.
Think: In what ways are you "crippled" like Mephibosheth?
Pray: Thank God for his grace and ask for help showing that grace to other "cripples" in your life.

DAY 33
EDGING GOD OUT

I read about a man in Pennsylvania who insisted on representing himself before the court after being charged with drunk driving. He told the judge the state laws didn't apply to him because, he said, "I live inside myself, not in Pennsylvania," and therefore he was a sovereign country that couldn't be prosecuted.

The judge decided the man needed a psychological evaluation.

Ya think?

Here's the sad thing: Most of us feel the same way. The only difference between this man and the rest of us is that this man said it out loud!

Let's admit it. We behave like we're a sovereign country, independent of everyone else around us. We let our desires take precedence over any consideration of others.

Pride is at the root of everything that ruins us. Think about it. Why do people go to their grave refusing to admit their lives could ever be so sinful that they would need Jesus to save them? Why do we put ourselves into deep debt and even live on God's tithe in order to put ourselves in houses, clothing, cars, and schools that impress others? Why do people neglect to pray, assuming their own wits can get them by? Why do people look away from the way God has commanded them to live and form their own version of morality? Why do we look smugly on someone else's sins, thinking we are somehow beyond the reach of sin ourselves? When we do fall into sin, why do we refuse to bring it to God so things can be set straight again?

The answer to all those questions: Pride.

There is an interesting little verse in the instructions on how to choose a pastor. First Timothy 3:6 says, "He must not be a recent convert, or he may become conceited and fall under the same judgment as the devil." That little verse is telling us that when we get conceited or puffed up with pride, we are re-enacting the same sin that brought down the devil.

Ken Blanchard, co-author of the One-Minute Manager and many other books on leadership, wrote, "The biggest addiction we have to overcome is the human ego. Why? Because ego stands for Edging God Out."

Let's not edge God out as we go through life today.

Read: James 4:1-10.
Think: Why is pride such a deadly sin?
Pray: Ask God to show you the advantages of living in humility.

DAY 34
HERE I AM

I first heard the song in a mall. Faintly above the din of shoppers' voices, I heard the voice of Emmylou Harris on the mall speakers...

I am standing by the river
I will be standing here forever
Though you're on the other side
My face you still can see
Why won't you look at me?

Here I am . . . Here I am . . .

I stopped and got out of the flow of shoppers to hear more. Clearly, this wasn't a typical love song. I was hearing God calling out to Adam and Eve -- and their progeny:

I am in the blood of your heart
The breath of your lungs
Why do you run for cover?
You are from the dirt of the earth
And the kiss of my mouth
I have always been your lover.
Here I am . . . Here I am . . .

I looked around the mall sure that someone else was hearing this, too. But the crowds shuffled by unmindful of the call. While they gazed in shop windows, licked dripping ice cream cones, talked to each other or messaged on their phones, the appeal continued:

I am the promise never broken
And my arms are ever open
In this harbor calm and still
I will wait until
Until you come to me

Here I am . . . Here I am . . .

"I'm not a particularly religious person," Harris wrote about her song. "But I thought, 'What must God be feeling when people just completely ignore Him?'"

Of course, mall music isn't meant to arrest shoppers' attention. I normally don't catch the music played in the background at a shopping center, either. But that day at the mall, I looked around at people oblivious to this love song that had captured my attention -- God's love song to his children. And the whole experience took on a powerful symbolism.

Each believer has a story of how they heard that divine call above the noise and distractions of their lives. We heard God say "Return to me!" and we gratefully responded.

Read: Revelation 3:20
Think: What is Jesus telling us when he promises "I will come in and eat" with us when we open the door to him?
Pray: Thank Jesus for knocking on the door of your heart and entering. Or ask Jesus to enter in if you haven't done so.

DAY 35
LOL WITH GOD

"Your great aunt passed away. LOL."

When a son got this text from his mother, he was baffled. "Why is that funny?" he asked.

His mom replied, "What do you mean, David. It's certainly not funny."

"Mom. LOL means 'Laughing Out Loud'."

"Oh my goodness! I sent that text to everyone! I thought it meant 'Lots of Love'!"

When was the last time you "laughed out loud" in wonder over God's goodness?

In Genesis 18, in the guise of a traveling stranger, God announced that the son he had promised Abraham 13 years earlier would finally be born before the next year. His wife, Sarah, overheard this and laughed bitterly to herself. She had given up on God long ago, and her laughter was a sign of her cynicism.

But in Genesis 21, Sarah held her little boy in her arms and laughed again. This time, though, she laughed with God, not at him. She named her son "Isaac" and exclaimed, "God has brought me laughter!"

You see, Isaac is a Hebrew word that means, well, "LOL"!

We shouldn't laugh at God's promises in cynical despair, but be sure to laugh with God when he keeps his promises.

Has God answered a prayer? LOL!

Has he surprised you with blessing? LOL!

Has he set you free from a destructive addiction? LOL!

Has he come through for you when you were at your wits end? LOL!

Has he rescued a marriage on the brink? LOL!

Has he given you the hope of eternal joy? LOL!

Singing, praying, giving -- they're all good acts of worship. But don't forget that laughing in wonder is worship, too!

Read: Psalm 126:1-3
Think: Think about a time someone laughed at you in derision. How did it feel? Do you think God feels that way when we respond with cynicism to his promises?
Pray: Thank God for as many answered prayers as you can think of.

DAY 36
SOLVING A "CRITICAL" PROBLEM

We need to learn how to *critique* without being *critical*.

How's that for a tough order? Jesus commanded this balance in back-to-back instructions found in Matthew 7:1-6. In verse 1, he began by saying, "Do not judge, or you too will be judged." And yet he turned right around in verse 6 to say, "Do not give dogs what is sacred; do not throw your pearls to pigs. If you do, they may trample them under their feet, and turn and tear you to pieces."

In other words, "Don't be judgmental, but do use good judgment!"

On the one hand, he doesn't want to see any scowling faces of condemnation among his followers. In one episode of *The Simpsons*, Homer sees his born-again neighbor, Maude Flanders. "Hey, I haven't seen you in a couple of weeks. Where have you been?" Maude replies, "Oh, I've been away at a Bible camp, learning to be more judgmental."

Ouch.

On the other hand, we need to exercise *more* discernment, not less. The legendary baseball player, Ted Williams, had such an intuition for the way a bat was supposed to feel that he once returned to the maker a batch of his Louisville Sluggers because he sensed that the handles were not quite right. It was discovered that the handles were off by five-thousandths of an inch. And when once challenged to find from among six bats the one that was half an ounce heavier than the others, he quickly did. Jesus wants us to develop that kind of intuition when it comes to moral evaluations.

So, can we improve our ability to discern what is morally "off" without falling into sour judgmentalism? And, on the other hand, can we quit being judgmental without also weakening our moral insight?

I can't think of a more important balance for our day. On the one hand, some of us feel like all of society will collapse if we don't respond to every issue that concerns us by picketing, protesting, and complaining of our offense in posts on social media. On the other hand, some of us can't seem to champion the virtue of tolerance without losing all ability to make any moral discernment at all.

Let's pursue the balance in this area that Jesus called for. Learn how to *make judgments* without being *judgmental*.

Read: Matthew 7:1-6
Think: Jesus expects us to be *discerning* and yet not *judgmental*. What are the consequences if we just make sure we're not judgmental and yet also fail to be discerning?
Pray: Ask God to help you be discerning and yet free of judgmentalism.

DAY 37
ANGER MANAGEMENT

Few United States governors will ever be as immortalized in popular culture as the late Alabama populist, George C. Wallace. The rock band Lynyrd Skynrd praised him in Sweet Home Alabama ("In Birmingham they love the guv-nah!"). And in the film, *Forrest Gump*, Wallace was introduced to new generations for his infamous stand at the school house door, attempting to block blacks from admission to the University of Alabama in 1963.

In fact, the Forrest Gump news footage is the only picture most people have of the Governor today: A defiant obstructionist with jutted jaw and curled lip, shouting "Segregation forever!"

But there's another picture of Wallace. While campaigning for president in 1972, Wallace survived an assassination attempt; but the bullet fired into him left him paralyzed in the legs. His brush with death got him to thinking about eternity, and he gave his life to Christ in 1983.

As the heavenly Ruler began to influence him, the earthly ruler began to change. One day, Wallace appeared unannounced at the Dexter Avenue Baptist Church in Montgomery, Alabama. This is the church Martin Luther King, Jr., was pastoring when he launched the civil rights movement in the 50s. Mr. Wallace wheeled his way to the front of the church where three hundred black ministers were concluding a day-long conference.

A hush fell over the crowd.

"I never had hate in my heart for any person," he said, "but I regret my support of segregation and the pain it caused the black people of our state and nation." Amid cries of "amen" and "yes, Lord," he continued. "Segregation was wrong, and I am sorry."

Two images of George Wallace. Hopefully the enduring image will not be the segregationist but the humbled, wheelchair-bound penitent, saying "I was wrong, and I am sorry."

Jesus said, "Settle matters quickly with your adversary. Do it while you are still with him on the way [to judgment]" (Matthew 5:25). The last and lasting image you want to bring before the throne of God is that of a humbled penitent saying to the one you hurt, "I was wrong, and I am sorry."

Read: Matthew 5:21-26
Think: Who do you need to go to and "settle matters quickly"?
Pray: It takes wisdom and courage to settle matters with another person. Ask for wisdom and courage.

DAY 38
PASSION AGAIN

A few years ago, a job placement service ran a Super Bowl ad with children talking about what they want to be when they grow up.

A boy said, "When I grow up, I want to file all day." Another child said, "I want to claw my way up to middle management." Still another boy said, "When I grow up, I want to be underappreciated." A girl said, "I want to be paid less for doing the same job." The last boy said, "I want to be forced into early retirement," and the spot faded to black, with the question superimposed, "What did you want to be?"

The commercial was so effective because it touched on the disconnect some of us have between what we wanted to be and what we are.

Let me play off that line. When you became a new believer, I doubt you said:

"In the future, I hope to lose all interest in prayer."

"I want staying current with my TV shows to be more important to me than influencing people's lives."

"I hope to complain and groan more than I do now."

"I want to lose my passion for working in God's service."

I doubt that was what you thought about in those days and months following your conversion. No, I think that when you first committed your life to Christ, your days were filled with purpose and dreams and expectancy and energy. I'm sure you were willing to rearrange anything and everything about your life in order to please God.

Since that time, though, some ask, "What happened? My fire has died down, my passion has faded."

My passion for God rises and falls. At times, I burn intensely for him: I consume his word like food, I pray expecting miracles, and I share my faith without hesitation. But at other times, the passion cools. I coast. My prayers go flat. I turn inward in self-pity.

I bet that's your story, too.

Colossians 2:6-7 tells us how to fan our faith into flame again: "So then, just as you received Christ Jesus as Lord, continue to live in him, rooted and built up in him, strengthened in the faith as you were taught, and overflowing with thankfulness."

Follow that route into new passion for Christ's cause.

Read: Colossians 2:6-7
Think: Recall those first few weeks and months after you first committed to Christ. Compare it to the passion you feel for him now.
Pray: Ask God to fan your faith into flame again.

DAY 39
WHAT IMPRESSION ARE YOU MAKING?

I read about sandals with treads that leave the words "Jesus" and "Loves You" as you walk along sandy or muddy ground. The sandals can be ordered for about $25 from a website called "Shoes of the Fishermen." The company also sells snowboots for those who want to leave their mark while walking in the snow.

I'll leave it up to you to decide if this is a worthwhile use of your money. But as I read the story about sandals that leave the words "Jesus Loves You" wherever the owner walks, it made me think. I couldn't help but ask what kind of "impression" I'm making in the lives of others.

In 1 Thessalonians 2:8 Paul said, "We loved you so much that we were delighted to share with you not only the gospel of God but our lives as well, because you had become so dear to us." I've memorized that verse, and you should, too.

Paul said he shared two things with them. First, he shared the gospel with them. He wanted them to know Jesus, to know Jesus' forgiveness and guidance and power for living. But Paul said he shared not only the gospel with them but also his life: his time, his energy, his heart. He was enthusiastically connected with them.

You go to enough churches enough times and you'll hear a challenge to share the gospel. The problem for too many of us is that even if we finally get up the nerve to share the gospel, we're hardly effective because we're not sharing the other thing that Paul listed: We're not sharing our lives with them.

Maybe the missing ingredient that keeps us from being effective witnesses is friendship. We need to nurture authentic relationships with those who need the Lord. Mark Mittleberg of Willow Creek Church calls it the "Barbeque First Principle." Invite them to a barbeque in your backyard before you invite them to church. In other words, socialize, be real, develop a no-strings-attached friendship with those around you.

You can buy some sandals that leave the Christian message as an impression in the sand, I suppose. But what are you doing to leave the Christian message as an impression in someone's life?

Read: 1 Thessalonians 2:8
Think: In what ways can you share your life with others in hopes of earning the right to share your gospel?
Pray: Ask God to bless your plans to build relationships with non-believers in the next few months.

DAY 40
TRUSTING GOD'S ABUNDANCE

I guess it's not easy to cash a check from God.

Maybe you missed the story of the 21-year-old who was arrested at an Indiana bank after he tried to cash a check for $50,000 that was signed "King Savior, King of Kings, Lord of Lords, Servant."

Upon his arrest for bank fraud, a felony, authorities found several other checks that were signed the same way but made out in different dollar amounts, including one for $100,000.

Last I heard, he was being held on a $1,000 bond.

And, no, the court wouldn't take a check.

Now, this isn't really a devotional about curious bank transactions. This is a devotional about prayer. And on that subject, our God really does offer some sizeable checks to his people. Jesus said, "Ask and it will be given to you; seek and you will find; knock and the door will be opened to you" (Luke 11:5-13).

Our prayers don't always reflect that confidence. Instead, we assess the data and calculate the odds and then bring a request to God that we think is within reason. That's why I can identify with the story in Acts 12. Herod had arrested Simon Peter with plans to execute him, "but the church was earnestly praying to God for him" (verse 5). When an angel miraculously rescued the church leader, Peter arrived at a home "where many people had gathered and were praying." He knocked, and when the servant girl heard his voice, she exclaimed to the prayer circle, "Peter is at the door!"

Their reply? "You're out of your mind."

Yep. The church that had witnessed so many miracles couldn't believe it when God answered their prayers for Peter.

We can be a lot like the folks in Acts 12. We're often more prepared for God to say "no" than for God to say "yes" when we pray to him.

Don't get me wrong. God doesn't say "yes" to our every prayer, and we need to learn to trust him when our requests are turned down. But I think we disappoint God when we decide ahead of time what kind of requests match his ability and willingness. Ephesians 3:20 says that God is "able to do immeasurably more than all we ask or imagine."

And you can take that to the bank.

Read: Acts 12:1-17
Think: As this 40-day devotional ends, what is the most significant truth and the most significant commitment you've made?
Pray: Ask God to make you bolder in praying to him and bolder in living for him.

ABOUT THE AUTHOR

For thirty-five years Tom Goodman has discussed faith with seekers and believers while serving as a pastor in Louisiana, the Cayman Islands, and Texas. He is a graduate of Baylor University and Southwestern Seminary in Texas, with a doctorate from New Orleans Seminary. He and his wife, Diane, have two sons. He enjoys scuba diving, fly fishing, and puttering around his wood-working shop. Tom blogs at www.anchorcourse.org/blog.